WITCH COVENS AND THE GRAND MASTERS

THE WITCHES' JOURNEY TO THE SABBAT, AND THE SABBAT ORGY

By

MONTAGUE SUMMERS

This edition published by Read Books Ltd.
Copyright © 2019 Read Books Ltd.
This book is copyright and may not be
reproduced or copied in any way without
the express permission of the publisher in writing

British Library Cataloguing-in-Publication Data
A catalogue record for this book is available
from the British Library

CONTENTS

Montague Summers 5

THE WITCHES' JOURNEY TO THE SABBAT, AND THE SABBAT ORGY................................ 7

Montague Summers

Augustus Montague Summers was born in Bristol, England in 1880. He was raised as an evangelical Anglican in a wealthy family, and studied at Clifton College before reading theology at Trinity College, Oxford with the intention of becoming a Church of England priest. In 1905, he graduated with fourth-class honours, and went on to continue his religious training at the Lichfield Theological College. Summers entered his apprenticeship as a curate in the diocese of Bitton near Bristol, but rumours of an interest in Satanism and accusations of sexual misconduct with young boys led to him being cut off; a scandal which dogged him his whole life. Summers joined the growing ranks of English men of letters interested in medievalism and the occult. In 1909, he converted to Catholicism and shortly thereafter he began passing himself off as a Catholic priest, the legitimacy of which was disputed. Around this time, Summers adopted a curious attire which included a sweeping black cape and a silver-topped cane.

Summers eventually managed to make a living as a full-time writer. He was interested in the theatre of the seventeenth century, particularly that of the English Restoration, and was one of the founder members of The Phoenix, a society that performed neglected works of that era. In 1916, he was elected a fellow of the Royal Society of Literature. Summers also produced some important studies of Gothic fiction. However, his interest in the occult never waned, and in 1928, around the time he was acquainted with Aleister Crowley, he published the first English translation of Heinrich Kramer and James Sprenger's *Malleus Maleficarum* ('*The Hammer of Witches*'), a 15th century Latin text on the hunting of witches. Summers then turned to vampires, producing *The Vampire: His Kith and Kin* (1928) and

The Vampire in Europe (1929), and then to werewolves with *The Werewolf* (1933). Summers' work on the occult is known for his unusual, archaic writing style, his intimate style of narration, and his purported belief in the reality of the subjects he treats.

In his day, Summers was a renowned eccentric; *The Times* called him "*in every way a 'character'" and "a throwback to the Middle Ages.*" He died at his home in Richmond, Surrey.

WITCH COVENS AND THE GRAND MASTERS

THE WITCHES' JOURNEY TO THE SABBAT, AND THE SABBAT ORGY

So vile and pestilent a superstition, whose evil and reprobate adherents the common consent of society holds as enemies to general order and, indeed, the foes of the human race. —POPE JOHN XXII.

Satan calleth them together into a Devilish Synagogue, and that he may also understand of them how well and diligently they have fulfilled their office of intoxicating committed unto them, and whom they have slain.
—LAMBERT DANEAU.

The dark and secret Society of Witches spreads—a huge network of evil—over the whole world. Throughout Europe and America in particular the organization of Satanists is very thorough and very complete. In less than the span of a limited lifetime, not more than sixty years indeed after the first settlers had landed at Massachusetts Bay, Cotton Mather notes as a detail significantly dangerous in itself and worthy of particular attention the systematic and methodized federation of the Salem witches. He says, " 'Tis very Remarkable to see what an Impious and Impudent *imitation* of Divine Things is Apishly affected by the Devil," and after showing that in many striking incidents the sorceries of the native Indians might be taken to be a burlesque of the Biblical narrative, he continues: "The Devil which *then* thus imitated what was in the Church of the *Old Testament*, now among *Us* would Imitate the Affairs of the Church in the *New*. The *Witches* do say, that they form themselves much after the manner of *Congregational Churches*; and that they have a *Baptism* and a *Supper*, and *Officers* among them, abominably Resembling those of our Lord."

There are, it is true, cases upon record and instances to be met with to-day of the solitary witch, dwelling apart and alone in some remote and unfrequented corner, apparently leading an almost isolated and eremitical life, but this is a rather rare exception.

The members of the witch society in various districts, large or small, villages, towns, great cities, or even shires and provinces, are linked up, and a correspondence is maintained between them in many mysterious ways. There is an active freemasonry of evil.

One of the oaths demanded from a novice is generally a pledge to frequent the midnight assemblies. These conventicles or *covens* are the meetings of bands or companies of witches summoned and forgathering under the discipline of an officer, who naturally was assisted in his work by other functionaries. Obviously the members of a coven would all belong as nearly as possible to the same neighbourhood, and especially was this the case in former years when the means of transit were far more slow and difficult than at the present day. It appears from the evidence at numerous trials, both at home and abroad, that those who belonged to a coven were bound to attend the weekly Esbat or rendezvous. The arrest of one member of a coven often led to the implication of many more who belonged to the same gang.

The number of witches which constituted and still constitutes a coven has been much discussed. In a famous Scotch trial of 1662 when the revelations of Isobel Gowdie, of Auldearne, gave the fullest details concerning almost every circumstance of witchcraft, amply describing the Sabbats, the minor meetings, the ceremonies and instructions in malefic charms, she confessed "ther ar threttin persons in ilk Coeven". In a very exhaustive investigation of this point Mr. Alexander Keiller thus sums up: "To those unaware of the probable organization of what might be termed the Witch Sect in Europe, in at any rate the sixteenth and seventeenth centuries, it may be explained that the Administrative and Executive Unit of Witchcraft customarily consisted of thirteen persons, and was usually termed a 'Coven' or 'Coeven'." This scholar has explored in great detail "The Territorial Distribution of Witchcraft in Aberdeenshire", and he has also set forth "The Personnel of the Aberdeenshire Witchcraft Covens in the years 1596–7" showing that there were five distinct covens each formed of thirteen members, as well as three other covens which owing to the lack of necessary data cannot be precisely completed.

Until at least the latter part of the seventeenth century a well-organized group of witches existed between Shotley Bridge and Corbridge in the county of Northumberland. Ann Armstrong a farm servant at Burtree House, a few miles from Stocksfield-on-Tyne, was for a time partially drawn into the society and when in February, 1672–3, she voluntarily deposed before a number of magistrates her witness was most clear and detailed. Lieut.-Colonel G. R. B. Spain writes: "It is obvious from the evidence that Ann Armstrong was closely in touch with a witchcraft organization over a large district of some fifty square miles." ("The Witches of Riding Mill, 1673": *Cornhill Magazine*, March, 1929.) Ann Armstrong described how the witches were divided into "coveys, consisting of thirteen persons in every covey".

On the other hand it can be equally well shown that in many cases the local group or coven of witches did not consist of thirteen members. Sixteen witches belonged to the St. Osyth coven in 1582; ten witches formed the coven that infested the Waltham and Hedingham countryside five years later. The witches of Warboys who so plagued the Throgmbrtons and killed Lady Cromwell were three in number. No less than thirty-five witches can be traced in connexion with the famous Pendle Forest trials (1613). To attempt to divide this total into covens of thirteen is singularly futile. In the effort to do so not only has evidence been juggled, but Mother Demdike and Mother Chattox are placed in the same group, upon which Mr. L'Estrange Ewen justly comments: "This is a wild argument. Demdike and Chattox could not have been in the same coven because they were very keen rivals." Some of the London covens of Satanists to-day are composed of as many as thirty or forty men and women; other circles again are quite small and only comprise ten initiates.

The *Officers* among the witches, of whom Cotton Mather speaks, were in the first place the local Chiefs or Masters of a coven, above whom was the Grand Master of a district.

There is very ample proof that "the Devil" of the Sabbat was not infrequently a human being, none other indeed than the Grand Master of the district, and since his officers and immediate attendants were also termed "Devils" by the witches some confusion has on occasion ensued. In Jersey the Grand Master, the Devil's deputy, was known as "Le Tchéziot". In a few cases where sufficient details are given it is possible actually to identify "the Devil" by name.

During the trial in December, 1481, at Neuchatel, of Rolet Groschet, he confessed that when quite a lad he had been taken to a meeting of witches by Jaquet Duplan. Here he was welcomed by "the Devil", a tall dark man, named Robin, to whom he did homage and who made much of him. The second time Groschet went to a rendezvous of sorcerers the gathering was much smaller, and the president was Captain Hanchement, evidently a well-known figure in the town, by whom he was appointed the local messenger for the society, and he used to go up and down to the various witches' houses giving notice of the assemblies and other bad businesses. At another time he attended a meeting of some other covens than his own belonging to Vauxtravers a few leagues away, and here the Provost was Etienne Goynet.

In 1579 at Windsor there used to meet "within the backside of Master Dodges in the Pittes" a coven presided over by Father Rosimond, of Farnham. It has been too ingeniously suggested that Father Rosimond *alias* Osborne, whom Mother Stiles of the coven named as her "chief", was a priest. But, no, this "wise man" (as he is termed) was a widower with a daughter who proved wellnigh as versed in sorcery as himself.

It is true that sometimes a clergyman stands revealed as a high official among the witches. The Rev. George Burroughs, pastor at Wells, Maine, was accused by eight of the Salem witches "as being an head Actor at some of their Hellish Rendezvouses, and one who had the promise of being a King in Satan's Kingdom". He was often heard to brag "that he was a *Conjuror*, above the ordinary Rank of Witches", whilst several of the Satanists declared that "he was the Person who had Seduc'd, and Compell'd them into the snares of Witchcraft". Now it is established beyond all question that George Burroughs was the Grand Master of the district. Admittedly in the wave of extreme rationalism which so inexplicably swept over Massachusetts at the beginning of the eighteenth century the General Court reversed George Burroughs' attainder and awarded damages to his heirs, but this does not in the least (as a recent historian appears to think) clear him from the guilt of witchcraft nor yet does it rebut even one particular of the charges which were proven up to the hilt again and again. Cotton Mather, for example, never altered his opinion of Burrough's culpability, and did not spare to express his sternest disapproval of the general *volte-face*.

Among a list of "confederates against Her Majesty Queen Elizabeth, who have diverse and sundry times conspired her life" we have Lord Paget, Sir George Hastings, Sir Thomas Hanmer, "Ould Birtles the great devel, Darnally the sorceror, Maude Two-good enchantresse, the ould witehe of Ramsbury, several other ould witches." Full details are lacking but it seems plain that Old Birtles was the Grand Master or "Devil" of a coven of Wiltshire Witches.

The evil William, Lord Soulis, of Hermitage Castle, often known as "Red Cap", was "the Devil" of a coven of sorcerers. He was protected by a terrible charm against any injury from rope or steel; cords could not bind nor sword pierce him. And so when he was seized by his enemies they rolled him up in sheets of lead and boiled him to death at a place called the Nine-Stane Rig.

> On a circle of stones they placed the pot,
> On a circle of stones but barely nine;
> They heated it red and fiery hot,
> And the burnished brass did glimmer and shine.
> They rolled him up in a sheet of lead
> A sheet of lead for a funeral pall;
> They plunged him into the cauldron red,
> And melted him body, lead, bones and all.

The chamberlain and chief counsellor of Philip IV of France, Enguerrand de Marigny, was a Grand Master of sorcerers prominent among whom were a notorious warlock, Jacobus de Lor, his wife and manservant. Jacobus killed himself in prison whilst awaiting trial; the witch, his wife, perished at the stake. Under Louis X, on 30th April, 1315, de Marigny was hanged at Paris.

An even more mysterious figure was Robert III d'Artois, the Grand Master of a veritable legion of witches. During the year 1333 he endeavoured to kill Philip VI, the Queen, and the Dauphin by his spells and enchantments. The design, before it could be matured, was betrayed by one of his minions, and proscription and sentence of perpetual banishment being pronounced against him, he fled to England where he proved powerful enough to stir up Edward III against France, and to his influence may be immediately ascribed the outbreak of the Hundred Years War. He was feared and shunned everywhere as a past master of image magic, and it was also whispered that he possessed a number of most impious manuscripts of goety written by Moorish sorcerers.

From these two instances, Enguerrand de Marigny and Robert III d'Artois, we see that the activity of the Witch society was no mere piece of casual mischief wrought by doting village crones, who harmed their neighbours and scattered domestic ills and unhappiness,—bad businesses enough—but it reached further and meddled with the highest politics to the confusion of kingdoms and the ruin of dynasties. Such, as we fearfully realize when we look at the world around us is its chief business, wherein it is fatally energetic and alive to-day. To reduce the world to a chaos of blood and horror; to stamp out and destroy all that is beautiful, all that has some reflection of God; such are the aims and object of the Red and the Witch.

One of the most interesting identifications of "the Devil" occurs in the course of the notorious trials of Geillis Duncan, Agnes Sampson, Dr. John Fian, and their associates in 1590–1. As is well known, the whole crew was in league with Francis Stewart, Earl of Bothwell, an incendiary vehemently suspected of the black art. Long after when George Sandys was staying at Naples there came to the inn a Calabrian, an eminent scholar, who insisted on seeing the English traveller. "And he," writes Sandys, "would needs persuade me that I had insight in magick: for that Earle *Bothel* was my countryman, who lives at *Naples*, and is in these parts famous for suspected negro-mancie." In Scotland, Bothwell, then a young man, was almost overtly aiming at the throne, and the witch covens one and all were frantically attempting the life of King James. Agnes Sampson, "the eldest witch of them all," confessed that she had fashioned a waxen puppet, and baptized it saying: "This is King James the Sixth, ordained to be consumed at the instance of a noble man, Francis, Earl Bothwell." At the next rendezvous of witches the presiding "Devil" anxiously questioned her concerning the moulding of the image, and what effect had followed the melting of the figure at a slow fire and the piercing of it with great black pins. There can be no doubt at all that Bothwell was the moving force who energized and directed the very elaborate and numerous organization of demonolaters who were attacking the King, seeking both his crown and his life. Bothwell was in fine the Grand Master, the "Devil" of the witches, and the centre of a vast political plot.

In the nineteenth century both Albert Pike and his successor Adriano Lemmi have been identified upon abundant authority as being Grand Masters of societies practising Satanism, and as performing the hierarchical functions of "the Devil" at the modern Sabbat.

In his *Displaying of Supposed Witchcraft*, 1677, John Webster had suggested with reference to Margaret Agar and other "*deluded Haggs*" of the Brewham coven, tried at Taunton during the June, Assizes of 1665, that the "little Man in black Clothes with a little band" who presided over the meeting at Hussey's Knap, a coppice near the hamlet, and who instructed the crew in moulding wax figurines and pricking them with thorns was the local Grand Master, a man-Devil, and Burns Begg points out that the witches on occasion "seem to have been undoubtedly the victims of unscrupulous and designing knaves, who personated Satan". This, however, is no palliation of their crimes, and they are not one whit the less guilty of sorcery and devil-worship if they obey and adore a representative of Satan, rather than the demon himself. Nor do I think that the man who personated Satan at these horrid assemblies was so much an unscrupulous and designing knave as himself a demonist, believing intensely in the reality of his own dark powers, wholly and horribly dedicated and doomed to the service of evil.

Moreover sometimes the demon himself appeared whilst the rites were in full blast, as at the horrible mockery of the Last Supper attended one Good Friday by Madeleine Bavent when Mathurin Picard was the celebrant of those blasphemies, and during this abominable supper a dark familiar walked round the table at which the company were seated, crying aloud: *Mot one of you shall betray me!*

God, so far as His ordinary presence and action in Nature are concerned, is hidden behind the veil of secondary causes, and when God's ape, the Demon, can work so successfully and obtain not merely devoted adherents but fervent worshippers by human agency, there is plainly no need for him to manifest himself in person either to particular individuals or at every Sabbat. None the less it is certain that he can do so, that he has done and yet does so very frequently, and the number of cases in the records of trials which are to be explained in no other way, that is to say where the devil manifests himself in some shape, appears to and has most intimate connexions with his besotted worshippers, are extremely numerous, and from what I know I am persuaded that we may safely avouch that to-day the demon is more frequently himself present at the modern sabbats than he functions through a deputy.

In the Caverne des Trois Frères, Ariège, France, there is depicted on the upper wall of the cave by some Palæolithic artist ten thousand years ago the figure of a man clothed in the skin of a stag with a horse's tail and wearing on his head huge branching antlers. This Caverne has a gallery of over four hundred pictures, but this figure "The Sorcerer" at the far end, painted high up on the rock in the "wizard's chamber", as it has been called, dominates the whole. Here then we have a masked magician, a Grand Master of the Old Stone Age.

A whole catena of evidence from the Fathers and Doctors of the Church might be easily adduced, all sternly denunciatory of those who dress themselves in the hides of animals and don great horns, thus decked out for licentious and profane assemblies and the performance of obscenest rituals. Thus St. Cæsarius of Arles (470–542) more than once anathematizes those who dress themselves in furry pelts and who don horned helmets, completely metamorphosed into animals. He warns the faithful: "If ye abhor any participation in their sins, ye will not suffer these human stags or bull-calves or other monsters to approach you, nay, not so much as to come nigh your dwellings."

Prohibitions of these devilish mummeries and bestial vizardings are to be repeatedly found in the early Penitentials.

We are forcibly reminded, and indeed there is a most intimate and vital connexion between the two, of the fiendish masks and dresses assumed by the witch-doctors and sorcerers of Africa and Tibet.

There is complete evidence that the hierophant at the witches' Sabbat, when a human being played that role, generally wore this traditional disguise. Nay more, as regards the British Isles at least—and it seems clear that in other countries the habit was very similar—we possess a pictorial representation of "the Devil" as he appeared to his worshippers. During the famous Fian trials—to which reference has already been made—Agnes Sampson confessed: "The devil was clad in a black gown with a black hat upon his head.... His face was terrible, his nose like the beak of an eagle, great burning eyes; his hands and his legs were hairy, with claws upon his hands and feet like the griffin." In the pamphlet *Newes from Scotland, Declaring the Damnable life and death of Doctor Fian* we have a rough woodcut, repeated twice, which shows "the Devil" preaching from the North Berwick pulpit to the whole coven of witches, and allowing for the crudity of the draughtsman and a few unimportant differences of detail—the black gown and hat are not portrayed—the demon in the picture is exactly like the description Agnes Sampson gave. It must be remembered, too, that at the Sabbat she was in a state of morbid excitation, in part due to deep cups of heady wine, the time was midnight, the place a haunted old church, the only light a few flickering, candles that burned with a ghastly blue flame.

Now "the Devil" as he is shown in the *Newes from Scotland* illustration is precisely the Devil who appears upon the title-page of Middleton and Rowley's masque *The World tost at Tennis*, 4to, 1620. This woodcut presents an episode towards the end of the masque, and here the Devil in traditional disguise, a grim black hairy shape with huge beaked nose, monstrous claws, and the cloven hoofs of a griffin, in every particular fits the details so closely observed by Agnes Sampson. I have no doubt that the drawing for this masque was actually made in the theatre, for although this kind of costly and decorative entertainment was almost always designed for court or some great nobleman's house, we know that *The World tost at Tennis* was produced with considerable success on the public stage "By the Prince his Servants". The dress, then, of "the Devil" at the Sabbats seems frequently to have been of the nature of an elaborate theatrical costume, such as might perhaps have been found in the stock wardrobe of a rich playhouse at London, but which would have had no histrionic associations for provincial folk and even simpler rustics.

Lambert Daneau, whose *Les Sorciers* was translated in 1575 by Thomas Taylor as *A Dialogue of Witches*, says that the "witches acknowledge the Devil for their God, call upon him, pray to him, and trust in him", and when they assemble at their Sabbats, "they repeat the oath which they have given unto him in acknowledging him as their God."

From almost every witch-trial in every land evidence to this effect might be accumulated. The matter is perfectly plain, and it is futile to attempt to conceal or confuse the issue, the God of the witches is and was the Devil, "the wicked one," "that old serpent called the Devil, and Satan, which deceiveth the whole world," "the Prince of the power of the air, the spirit that now worketh in the children of disobedience," who "sinneth from the beginning", "a murderer from the beginning," "a liar, and the father of it." Be it remarked that these phrases are neither "cheap claptrap" nor "purple patches" nor swayed by colourful prejudice. I quote the simple unvarnished words of the Authorized Version of the English Bible.

On those occasions when no visible presence of discarnate evil, no demon, appeared or presided at the Sabbat orgy, divine honours were paid to Satan's deputy, the Grand Master, although it does not follow that he was in himself and of himself regarded as absolute God. It is a nice, but none the less an important distinction, and although essentially true I am not prepared to say that as such it was apprehended by the majority of the witches, assuredly not by the poorer and clownish folk from whom, in the British Isles at any rate, so many of the covens were recruited.

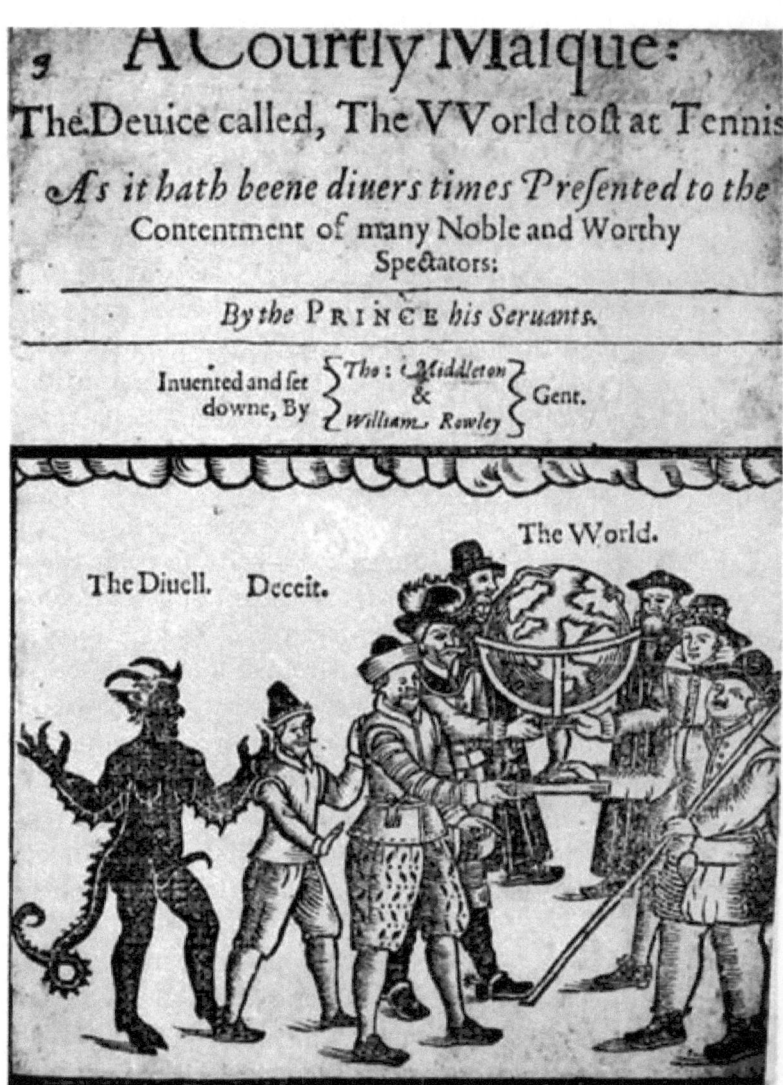

THE WORLD TOST AT TENNIS
The First Quarto

Among certain primitive peoples and in various savage tribes the chieftain or King was regarded as representative of and partaking in deity. He was, in fact, a man-god, and we find that very often he was ceremonially put to a violent death. As summed up by Sir James Frazer: "the motive for slaying a man-god is a fear lest with the enfeeblement of his body in sickness or old age his sacred spirit should suffer a corresponding decay, which might imperil the general course of nature and with it the existence of his worshippers who believe the cosmic energies to be mysteriously knit up with those of their human divinity." Such in brief is the theory of "The Dying God" or "The Divine Victim", as it is conveniently known.

It is a curious and irresponsible fantasy which attempts to superimpose the hypothesis of the "Divine Victim" upon the Grand Masters of the witches. Such a figment is difficult to be approached in serious discussion, since it offers no vestige of reality, and vaguely imaginative conjectures are not easy of refutation, or rather they carry their own disproof. Yet we are assured that certain figures, both historical and legendary, as for example King Edmund, the "deed-doer", King Edmund Ironside, King Cnut "the Great", Bishop Walcher of Durham, William Rufus, St. Thomas of Canterbury, St. Joan of Arc, Gilles de Rais, Robin Hood, Friar Tuck, were not only Grand Masters of witch societies, but also "the Incarnate God". Every one of these personages was ceremonially put to death, and the sacrifice was repeatedly consummated. When we venture to ask what tittle of fact exists to support this amazing assertion, we are coolly instructed that in the first place all records, all evidence from history must be swept aside as useless (a very necessary preliminary this, I am willing to admit), and "the Christian inquisitors are unanimous on this point", which last statement is, I venture to say, wholly unfounded. It really is not worth while—even if space allowed—to enter into all these cases in detail. I would merely point out that in the instance of St. Joan of Arc these wild theories have been dealt with by scholars and historians to be exploded once and for all. Nor would it be difficult to show how preposterous such fabling is with regard to the other names. The murder of William Rufus in the New Forest was due to homosexual jealousy, and although they have been squeamishly suppressed practically the full details of the affair can be traced. If anyone likes to consider that Robin Hood and Friar Tuck were wizards I hardly suppose that any serious objection will be raised, but I submit that it is distinctly offensive to very many when St. Thomas a Becket stands thus defamed. I am only too well aware that devotion to St. Thomas is weak and anaemic enough in England. It is a matter for regret that his holy Feast is not celebrated amongst us with greater solemnity, that his secondary Feast of the Translation is observed in only one diocese. Yet there are still those who visit Canterbury "The holy blisful martir for to seke". St. Thomas still has his clients who keep Tuesday in his honour, who have kissed the hallowed spot where he fell, who make pilgrimage and worship at his shrine.

In the case of historical figures the sole argument to show that such-an-one was a Grand Master of witches and "the Incarnate God" seems to be a violent death. I shall not be in the least surprised to be told that Jack Sheppard, Dick Turpin, Eugene Aram, George Barnwell and Sweeney Todd were "Incarnate Gods", whilst to companion Friar Tuck let us have Grindoff the Miller, Bill Sikes, Count Fosco and Cock Robin.

To quote a shrewd saying of the famous Dr. Henry More:

> "*At this pitch of wit . . . is the Reason of our professed Wit-would-be's of this present Age, who will catch at any slight occasion or pretence of misbeliving those things that they cannot endure should be true.*"

The name Sabbat, the derivation of which does not appear to be exactly established, may be held to cover almost every formal assembly of devil-worshippers, and thus ranges from comparative simplicity, the secret rendezvous in the open air or in some poor hut of half-a-dozen witches devoted to the fiend and presided over by the official of the village, to a large and crowded congregation adoring the demon upon his throne and marshalled by incarnate evil intelligences, a mob outvying the angels of the pit in malice, blasphemy, and revolt, the vomit of pandemonium on earth.

The day of the week whereon the Sabbat was held varied in different localities and at several times. There is indeed an accumulation of evidence for every night, although Friday was most generally favoured. Saturday and Sunday were if possible particularly avoided, especially a Saturday. At the trial of Louis Gaufridi in May, 1614, it was proved that the Sabbats were held on every night of the week. Wednesday and Friday were the Sabbats of blasphemy and the Black Mass, whilst to the other nights were allotted the most hideous villainies which humanity can conceive or perform. In England, it was stated during the seventeenth century that the "Solemn appointments and meetings . . . are ordinarily on Tuesday or Wednesday night". The witches of Burgundy met on Tuesday night, so we may conclude with Boguet "that there is no fixed day for the Sabbat, but that witches go to it whenever Satan so commands". This is confirmed by Madeleine Bavent who says: "There seemed to be no fixed day for the assembly."

Antide Colas confessed that she was wont to attend the Sabbat upon each of the greater Festivals of the year, as for example at Christmas, Easter, Corpus Christi, and Boguet gives us the reason for this too—"the wicked one celebrates his assemblies on Holy Days, and thus mockingly seduces the creatures of God from His service."

Thus we hear of Sabbats being held on the vigils of the "nine chief feasts of the year", namely, Easter, Epiphany, Ascension Day, the Purification, Nativity and Assumption of Our Lady, Corpus Christi, All Saints, and the Nativity of St. John Baptist. In one English village the Sabbat was held on St. Bartholomew's Eve, this apostle being Patron of the Church and parish. Throughout

Eastern Europe a Sabbat was held on the Eve of St. George. In Western Europe the day of one of the principal assemblies was on 30th April, the Eve of May Day, famous over all Northern Germany as Die Walpurgis-Nacht, the Night of Saint Walburga.

The Grand Sabbats were convened in a great variety of places, whilst the lesser Sabbats could be easily assembled in an even larger number of spots, as might be most convenient to the Satanists of the district, a field near a village, a wood, a tor, a valley, an open waste beneath some blasted oak, a cemetery, a ruined building, some solitary chapel or deserted church, and often in a house belonging to one of the initiates.

It was advisable that the selected locality should be remote to obviate any chance of espionage or casual interruption, and in many localities some wild ill-omened gully or the lone hill-top was shudderingly marked as the notorious haunt of witches and their fiends.

De Lancre says that in the Basque country the Grand Sabbat was invariably held near a stream, a lake, or water of some kind. Bodin confirms this to some extent, for Antoine Gandillon, a witch of long continuance, told him that there must always be water in the place of the Sabbat, and the little coven of the village of Coirières held their Sabbat near a mill-dam. The Breton witches assembled among the ancient cromlechs and ruined dolmens of their province. The market-crosses of sleepy old towns and English villages were among the favourite rendezvous of our country warlocks and witches. Mother Agar, the Brewham witch, and her company forgathered on Brewham Common, and also at Husseys-knap, a coppice just beyond the hamlet. Dr. Fian and his associates on All Hallows E'en assembled at the lonely and haunted church of North Berwick. Silvain Nevillon, who was executed at Orleans on the 4th February, 1615, confessed "that the Sabbat was celebrated in a house", and the full details which he gave shows this to have been a large château, no doubt the home of some wealthy local magnate, a Satanist and probably the Grand Master of the district, within whose walls above 200 persons could assemble.

In Jersey the witches' rendezvous was under the shadow of a large rock south of Rocqueberg Point, St. Clement, and it is believed that at their Sabbats they often raised storms which imperilled those at sea and drowned many a fisherman.

The Guernsey witches celebrated "the Feast of the Sabbat" on Friday nights on the hill of Catiôroc, around the cromlech called "Le Trépied". At the time of the full moon they also met near the mill which stands on the hill at Ville-ès-Pies. Their favourite spot, however, was the sands of Rocquaine Bay, where they used to perform obscene dances chanting a roundelay of which the burden ran "Qué-hou-hou! Marie Lihou!" words uttered in impious defiance and mockery of Notre Dame, Sainte Marie de Lihou. This was a spot of such extraordinary sanctity, that although both priory and church are but a heap of shapeless ruins even to-day the French coasting vessels as they pass salute it by lowering their topmast.

One of the most notorious meeting-places for witches was the Brocken, popularly known as the Blocksburg, the highest peak of the Hartz mountains. On Walpurgis Night huge assemblies of Satanists were wont to forgather there, some (it is said) coming from Norway and even from distant Lapland. Local Blocksburgs existed, or rather hills so called, especially in Pomerania which boasted two or three such crags.

Night was almost invariably the time for the Sabbat. Father Delrio aptly observes: "Their assemblies are generally held at dead of night when the Powers of Darkness reign; or, sometimes, at high noon, even as the Psalmist saith, when he speaks of 'the noonday devil'." The Lancashire witches celebrated their Sabbat "about twelve of the clock in the day time". The witches of Stoke Trister, near Wincanton, "met about nine of the Clock in the Night, in the Common near *Trister* Gate." Mother Bishop, a Somersetshire witch, confessed "That she hath been at several meetings in *Lie* Common, and at other places in the night". On one occasion Christian Green of Brewham and other witches met the devil "in *Brewham* Forest about Noon", but the coven more frequently used to assemble "at a place called *Husseys-knap* in the Forest in the Night time".

The time at which the Sabbat began was generally upon the stroke of midnight. It lasted until the cock crew, when everything vanished away.

A witch named Babilla Latoma, when minutely questioned by Nicolas Remy about the nightly doing of sorcerers, confessed that nothing was more fatally obstructive to their loathsome businesses than that a cock should crow. Two other witches informed the same judge that when it was time to break up their nocturnal assemblies the officers proclaimed in stentorian voices: "Ho! make haste and away, all; for the cock begins to crow." That the crowing of a cock dissolves enchantments is a tradition of remotest antiquity, and the poet Prudentius very beautifully sings how the night-wandering demons, who rejoice in dunnest shades, at the crowing of the cock tremble and scatter in sore affright.

It has been quite confidently and quite erroneously stated that in England the witches' Sabbat was practically unknown, or at most, when the evidence proves overwhelming and such as is impossible to slur or set aside, it is argued that the English Sabbat "was a feeble reflection of its foreign original", and existed only in an "attenuated" form. It is difficult in the face of facts which certainly cannot be dismissed and which one would have thought could hardly be misinterpreted to appreciate whence this fallacy arose, but since it has been so seriously put forward and maintained it becomes necessary to make specific mention of some few from the many cases in English witchcraft proving the Assemblies or "synagogues" of Satanists—and such gatherings continue very actively to-day—whereat every kind of mischief and devil's craft was hatched and ingeniously propelled.

In 1579 the Windsor coven which was presided over by Father Rosimond of Farnham were wont to assemble for their Sabbats "within the backside of Master Dodges in the Pittes", and also about eleven o'clock at night at the Pound. They were adepts in making figurines, and having moulded in red wax "pictures" of a neighbouring farmer and his maidservant, a local butcher, and the Mayor of Windsor, they killed these four persons by sorcery, piercing the figures through and through with sharp hawthorn spines and prickles. A very important Sabbat was held by the Lancashire witches on Good Friday, 1612, at Malking Tower, the abode of old Mother Demdike, where twenty and more indulged in a gluttonous orgy, and plotted no inconsiderable amount of mischief, including the murder of Thomas Lister, of Westly, which they very effectually contrived in less than two or three months. The Salmesbury witches, three of whom were put on their trial in the same year, 1612, used to celebrate their Sabbats on Thursday and Sunday nights on the banks of the Ribble, where they met four tall black men who provided meat and wine, who danced with them and fornicated. Two of the witches who had secretly killed a small child, after the burial of the body dug it up, boiled it in a pot and ate it, seething the bones to obtain fat for the witch's ointment.

Ten years later the witches who plagued the family of that eminent poet and scholar Edward Fairfax of Fewstone, in the Forest of Knaresborough, used to meet at midnight at Timble Gill, where a table was spread with food and flagons, and the Devil sat at the upper end.

In the case of the Second Lancashire witches, 1634, Margaret Johnson confessed that on the Sunday within the octave of All Saints she attended a Sabbat at a house called Hoarestones (which was still standing in 1845) and there were present about forty witches with their familiars. She further stated that Good Friday was "one of their constant days of their general meeting".

Matthew Hopkins relates that in 1644 when he was living at Manningtree, Essex, a number of witches, both of his own town and from neighbouring villages, "every six weeks in the night (being always on the Friday night) had their meeting close by his house, and had their several solemn sacrifices there offered to the Devil."

About the same year the Leicestershire witches used to forgather at Burton-on-the-Wolds "above four score" at a Sabbat, and at Tilbrooke bushes near Catworth "above twenty at one time" to worship and serve the demon.

In September, 1645, Goodwife Hott, a witch of Faversham, Kent, related how "there was a great meeting at Goodwife Pantery's house, and that Goodwife Dadson was there, and that Goodwife Gardner should have been there, but did not come, and the Devil sat at the upper end of the table".

Dr. Henry More, the famous Platonist philosopher, learned that a coven of witches held their Sabbats at the house of Mother Lendall of Cambridge, a woman most ill-famed for impiety and evil, and that here late at night the "table was well furnished with guests and meat", whilst at the head of the board there sat one in black to whom the numerous company louted low with great reverence and did obeisance. Much of the talk among the leaders of the party was carried on in a strange tongue, not understood of the humbler folk present.

The Malmesbury coven in 1671 celebrated their orgies at night in the house of one of the dark fellowship, and here they securely feasted and drank deeply and committed every kind of uncleanness, also plotting evilly enough against their enemies and planning murders with only too speedy and efficacious results.

The very dangerous and extremely well-organized society of witches who infested the Northumbrian woodlands and open moors between Shotley Bridge and Corbridge at the end of the seventeenth century had their general meeting-place at a house galled Riding House, near Riding Mill Bridge End, where there was a banquet spread and "their protector whom they called their god" sat at the top of the table in a great gilt chair. One Good Friday no less than sixty-five witches attended a great feast at the house of John Newton, of the Riding, near Riding Mill, where they were served with boiled capons, rich cheeses, butter, white bread, beef, bottles of rare wine, and a vast variety of all meats.

Another Sabbat was held at Allensford on the Derwent, when the whole coven danced their ritual measure. Yet another Sabbat was celebrated in the cellar of Master Francis Pye's house at Morpeth.

In Massachusetts whither the foul traditions of witchcraft had been brought from England and there could be no question of continental custom or influence, the Salem witches held their General Meetings and solemn Sabbat—"hellish Randezvouzes," Cotton Mather justly terms them—in a field not far from the village, and sometimes in a house belonging to a warlock who lived there. Here they celebrated a Sabbat on the very day a Public Fast was being kept on account of the sorceries and devilment which were so sorely plaguing the countryside. There were "Meetings, Feastings, Dancings" in other places as well, and a number of novices were baptized into this horrid society in the river at Newbury Falls.

At the risk of some slight repetition I have thought it well to give a catena extending over a century (1579–1692) to show beyond all quibble or question that the English witches assembled at set times and in set places for their formal Sabbats where every species of wickedness and devil-worship prevailed, and that there was in fine amongst them a definite and disciplined organization of the infernal cult of Satanism, which is one and the same the whole world over. It would not be difficult, moreover, to carry on the chain of evidence throughout the eighteenth and nineteenth centuries down to the London Sabbats of the present day.

I believe the point has been raised that the English Sabbats were but small gatherings in comparison with the large assemblies in Germany, in the Pyrenees, at Mohra in Sweden, in the Val Gamonica, at Benevento, and other places. It is true that the witches flocked in crowds to certain notorious centres, and when a district was widely infected with Satanism naturally the covens would be more numerous. Yet we hear of no less than twenty attending a Sabbat in the second case of the Lancashire witches; sixty-five were present at the Sabbat in John Newton's house, Riding Mill; whilst at the notorious Sabbat at North

Berwick church there assembled two hundred devil-worshippers, although, of course, strictly speaking this is not an English example. To-day also there are sometimes as many as twenty-five or thirty at a Sabbat. No doubt in villages such as Brewham the coven was few, but the Wincanton society numbered thirteen and perhaps more. Similar proportions seem to have prevailed (as we might reasonably expect) upon the continent.

The next detail which presents itself for inquiry is, how the witches reached the Sabbat? The answer seems at first glance simple enough: they ride, they drive, they go on foot, travelling in whatever way is most convenient. When Agnes Sampson, who lived at Keith, attended the midnight Sabbat at North Berwick church, "she passed there on horseback, conveyed by her godson, called John Cooper." When the Pendle witches assembled at Malking Tower, an extremely isolated and ancient stronghold which stood on the further slope of the high conical-shaped hill which shuts in Rough Lee glen to the north-east, they "gotten on Horsebacke", some mounting steeds of one colour, some of another. When Ann Armstrong, a servant of the Fowlers at Burtree House, near Stocks-field-on-Tyne, was taken to the Sabbat at Riding Mill Bridge End she saw the witches arrive on horseback. Their leader, whom they spoke of as "their protector", was "a long black man riding on a bay galloway", in other words a garran, a small stout Scotch horse. When the orgy was over the whole crew took the saddle again for home with their protector leading the party.

Major Thomas Weir, the Edinburgh warlock, and his sister Jean Weir, used to drive to the Sabbats at Musselburgh in a coach, and for more than a hundred years after the execution of these two miserable witches it was said that the rattling and thundering of a heavy coach could be heard at midnight over the cobbles as the phantom equipage whirled along by black steeds of hell passed swiftly down the Bow to halt before Weir's horrible house and then vanish in a flame of fire. It is probable that many hauntings by spectral coaches are to be explained thus, namely that the apparitions are those of wizards who were wont thus to travel to the Sabbat and whose foul ghosts still cling to the route they covered in life on evil bent again and again. A château not far from Morlaix in Brittany is fearfully haunted in this way. On certain anniversaries the windows of the empty house are illuminated from within as by numberless candles, the old cracked bell in the turret clangs harshly, and up the long drive there speeds an ancient coach within which are seated four shadowy figures. These are said to be a certain seigneur, lord of the manor in the early decades of the eighteenth century, his son and two grandsons, all of whom were Satanists, handing down the infernal tradition from scion to scion of their accursed line.

Early in the sixteenth century a gang of Satanists made their headquarters at Yarmouth, and it is plain that they were protected by certain great persons living in that district who belonged to the evil society. In the reign of Elizabeth six Yarmouth witches, including Elizabeth Butcher, a very active devil's agent, were hanged, and under Charles I another five witches were executed. Caister Castle near Yarmouth was formerly visited by a phantom coach which drove round the courtyard of the castle and halted, whereupon a number of dark muffled figures seem to emerge silently from various doorways and corners, and enter the vehicle. The door was slammed to with a horrible noise, the crack of a whip was heard, and the six headless black horses set off at full gallop. No doubt these were the spectres of the wizards doomed endlessly to repeat their journey to the unhallowed orgies of the Sabbat.

A similar coach haunts the roads near Langley Hall, Durham. Although it is true that many cases of witchcraft have not come to light in this district it may be noted that in January, 1651–1652, two notorious warlocks were executed at Durham, and it is more than probable that the organization had secretly taken root there, whilst the boggart coach is the phantom of that which was wont to convey certain sorcerers to their diabolic rendezvous.

Witches sometimes go on foot to the Sabbat, and this usually happens when the place of their assembly is not very distant from their homes. Thus Bernard of Como, a famous Dominican scholar, remarks that when witches are to attend the Sabbat at some spot hard by their dwellings, "they proceed thither on foot conversing as they go." When a Sabbat was celebrated in the field of Longchamois, the witches of Orcieres, about a quarter of a league away, walked thither in a party. The Wincanton witches walked to the Sabbat held on the common near Trister Gate, a bare couple of miles away, whilst for Mother Style of Stoke Trister it can only have been a matter of a few hundred yards.

A young Satanist, Isaac de Queyran, told Pierre De Lancre, the Bordeaux judge, that witches who dwelt at some distance flew home from the Sabbat through the air, whilst those whose houses were not far away returned on foot. De Lancre comments: "It is truly as criminal and abominable for a Sorcerer to go to the Sabbat on foot as to be voluntarily conveyed thither by the Devil."

In all the above cases (save truly in the hints given by de Queyran) the method of proceeding to the Sabbat proves perfectly commonplace and usual, but the witches also employed other means which were extraordinary and indeed preternatural. The popular imagination has seized upon one of these and often exaggerates it into something surpassingly fantastic and bizarre, for although the witch is universally credited with the power to fly through the air mounted upon a besom or some kind of stick it is remarkable in the face of so general and picturesque a belief to find that the confessions avowing this actual mode of aerial transport are comparatively few.

None the less it is significant that the belief in the nocturnal transport through the air of sorcerers, either bent on some malefic business or to attend their assemblies, is practically universal, and exists among savage races as strongly as amongst civilized people. In the Congo, for example, members of the secret society *Bwiti* during certain wizard ceremonies rise from the ground to a height of several feet during the space of a quarter of an hour. The Indians of North America credited their pow-wows with the faculty of raising their bodies from the ground for an appreciable length of time, and a French missionary, Father Papetard told Dr. Imbert-Gourbeyre, that whilst at Oregon he had himself seen more than once native warlocks levitate themselves two or three feet from the ground and walk upon the top of the blades of long pampas grasses without bending the tender panicles. In Australia, too, the native tribes such as the Boandik, West Arunta, Kurnai, and others are perfectly familiar with the aerial transport of magicians, who are said to be conveyed by ghosts, that is to say (as we know) by demons. In one of the tribes of the Wotjobaluk group an ancient seeress not infrequently "went up aloft, being supported, as it was believed, by ghosts [devils], from whom she gleaned information as to the dead". This is related together with many other striking examples by A. W. Howitt in his work on *The Native Tribes of South-East Australia*.

It stands to reason that Satan, the ape of God, must imitate and caricature the divine phenomenon of mystical levitation.

According to the great *Oxford English Dictionary* the word "levitation" does not date back before 1875. It was first employed in England, and in earliest use with reference to spiritualism (spiritism). Levitation means that the human body is able under certain conditions to be raised from the ground, and to remain for a longer or shorter space of time suspended in the air without any visible support, and not infrequently to move to and fro in the air without the apparent or traceable action of any physical forces.

In hagiography this is a recognized and not infrequent occurrence, and very many instances are noted by the Bollandists in their immense work on the Lives of the Saints. It is not too much to say that some hundreds of such cases have been known. There are the Scriptural examples of Enoch, Elijah, Habakkuk, S. Philip the Deacon, and the transports of Our Lord Himself, Whose earthly life was consummated in that supreme levitation we name the Ascension. There are the cases of early Saints, Saint Mary Magdalene, Saint Antony the Great, Saint

Mary of Egypt. There are the modern traditions of such great names as Saint Dominic, Saint Francis, Saint Bonaventura, Saint Thomas Aquinas, Saint Catherine of Siena, Saint Peter of Alcantara, Saint Teresa, Saint Philip Neri—to name almost at random only a very few. In the nineteenth century we have that glorious visionary and mystic Anne Catherine Emmerich; the Italian Maria Domenica Barbagli; the Curé d'Ars; Mary of Jesus who died in 1862, and whose levitations formed the subject of a report in a bulletin of the *Société des Sciences psychiques*; the Carmelite Sister Mary of Jesus Crucified who died at the Carmel of Bethlehem in 1878; an ecstatica living near Nantes, Marie Julie Jahenny, who is still alive.

Perhaps the two most famous examples of levitation are Saint Alphonsus Liguori and Saint Joseph of Copertino. Some of the raptures and upliftings of Saint Alphonsus were experienced in public, as in the church of Foggia in December, 1745, when as he was preaching he was raised to a height from the floor in the presence of a crowded congregation who could not refrain from crying aloud: "A miracle! a miracle!"

With regard to the Franciscan Joseph of Copertino, who died at the Conventual house at Osimo in September, 1663, his levitations and ecstatic flights through the air from one place to another were so frequent that the Bull of canonization says no Saint can be compared to him in this respect. His raptures in saying Mass were of daily occurrence, and for no less than thirty-five years his Superiors had to exercise the greatest caution, requiring him on certain feasts, especially those of Our Lady, to say Mass in a private oratory so that the religious "should not be disturbed by the concourse of the vulgar", many of whom came more from curiosity (it is to be feared) rather than devotion to see this marvellous mystic at the altar.

The evidence for the levitations of Saint Alphonsus and Saint Joseph (as indeed for very many other holy persons) has been sifted with the utmost thoroughness, and there is no room whatsoever left for doubt or question.

In this connexion we cannot neglect to remark upon mediumistic levitations, one of the most famous examples being the case of Daniel Dunglas Home, of whom Sir William Crookes bore witness: "On three separate occasions have I seen him raised completely from the floor of the room. . . . There are at least a hundred recorded instances of Mr. Home's rising from the ground. . . . The accumulated testimony establishing Mr. Home's levitations is overwhelming." In November, 1868, Lord Adare and Lord Lindsay saw Home raised four or five feet from the ground. At Ashley House, Home was carried out at one window and borne in through another at a height of 70 feet from the ground. Once at Adare Abbey, he floated swiftly for a space of twelve yards through the air. In a garden at Stockton he was aerially transported for more than a hundred feet.

William Stainton Moses was levitated six feet; Eusapia Palladino, on occasion from some inches to fully five feet; Mrs. French, a couple of feet; Maria Vollhart, one foot; whilst the Brazilian Carlos Mirabelli even when fastened to an armchair was levitated in the presence of several acutely observant members of the Academia Cesare Lombroso, remaining for several minutes suspended twelve feet from the ground so that the witnesses could pass and repass under the body tied to the chair. (It is by no means unusual for objects in contact with the levitated person to be similarly influenced by the phenomenon.) At Santos Mirabelli experienced levitation in the street, being uplifted from a motor car for about three minutes.

Now angels, be they blessed spirits or demons, have the power to move matter. The levitation of sorcerers is effected by the agency of evil forces, devils who bestow this favour upon an auxiliary and a companion.

Dr. John L. Nevius, of Chefoo, who was for forty years a missionary to the Chinese, in his study *Demon Possession* relates how certain Chinese wizards "are carried by invisible power from place to place. They ascend to a height of twenty or fifty feet, and are carried to a distance of four or five *li*". (A *li* is one-third of a mile.) The same phenomenon occurs in the case of European witches, who have been and are borne by the invisible power of Satan to the Sabbat, or it may be on some other errand of mischief and destruction.

Paul Grilland in his treatise *On Witchcraft*, published in 1533, speaks of a trial of a sorceress at Rome seven years before, at which he was present, and it was asserted that she flew in the air after she had anointed her limbs with a certain magic liniment. Some witches, says Boguet, use a mysterious ointment, and others use none. "Before they go to the Sabbat," writes Guazzo, "the witches anoint themselves on some part of their bodies with an unguent made from various foul and filthy ingredients, but chiefly from murdered children; and so anointed they are carried away on a cowl-staff, or a broom, or a reed, a cleft stick, or a distaff, or even a shovel, which things they ride."

Dr. Johann Weyer, in his treatise on witches, has transcribed certain formulae for the magical ointment. He tells how the witches boil the fat of babes in a brazen cauldron. They scum this thickly, and make it into a kind of grease, kneading into it a commixture of hemlock, aconite, poplar leaves, and soot. Another recipe is: Cowbane, sweet flag, cinquefoil, bat's blood, belladonna, and oil. There are, Weyer adds, other ointments, but the essential ingredients remain the same in all.

Collette Dumont, a Guernsey witch, who was executed in 1617, confessed that the Devil had given her a certain black ointment, with which, having stripped, she rubbed her body all over, and then again dressed and went out of doors when she was immediately borne through the air with incredible velocity to the appointed place for the Sabbat. This was sometimes near the Torteval parish churchyard, and sometimes on the seashore hard by Rocquaine Castle.

It is related that a certain Guernsey lady of St. Pierre-du-Bois becoming very suspicious of the long hours of retirement her husband passed in his own apartments was induced by curiosity to watch him. Accordingly one day she concealed herself in the room. He entered, and stripping himself naked anointed his limbs with a certain ointment, repeating the Words *va et vient*. He then seemed to disappear from sight. After a while she came forth, and went through the same ceremony, when in a twink she found herself on the summit of Pleinmont in the midst of a large company. A table was spread with costly viands, of which some who were present courteously invited her to partake. Crossing herself for her grace, she said *Au nom de Dieu soit, Amen*. No sooner had she spoken than all had disappeared, and the only signs of any beings having approached the spot were the recent marks of cloven feet which seemed to have scorched and trampled the sward in every direction.

In the *Malleus Maleficarum* it is explained at length how witches having anointed either themselves or some chair or broomstick with the devil's ointment can be and are transported up through the air about their master's business. Sometimes also they are carried on animals, which are not true animals but devils in that form. The witches too not unseldom appear to be metamorphosed into animals, especially cats. And this is merely glamour, a trick of the devil, who, Saint Thomas tells us, can entirely confuse and cheat the senses, so that a witch is persuaded she is changed into a cat, and those of her society see her as a cat, whereas it is all illusion.

"The commonest practice of all witches is to fly up through the chimney. If anyone objects that chimneys are too small and narrow, or raises any other difficulties, he must know that by virtue of that Demonolatry which makes all things monstrous and portentous, they are first bidden to exceed their natural limits; and moreover the matter becomes more intelligible when it is remembered that the chimneys are square and wide in all peasant's cottages, and it is from this class that the vile rabble of sorcery is mostly derived." In his account of the Swedish witches of 1669–1670, who were conveyed to Blockula, the place of the Sabbat, by diabolic agencies, Anthony Horneck says that, "Being asked how they could go with their Bodies through Chimneys and broken panes of Glass, they said, that the Devil did first remove all that might hinder them in their flight, and so they had room enough to go."

During the trial of the Somersetshire witch, Julian Cox, at the Taunton assizes, 1663, a "Witness swore that she had seen *Julian Cox* fly into her own Chamber Window in her full proportion, and that she very well knew her, and was sure it was she."

From these cases it is certain that witches are levitated and carried in this way to the Sabbat. The ointment is actually of no effect *per se*, and the devil can (and often will) transport sorcerers to the Sabbat without any smearing with unguent or lotions. The ointment is employed as a sort of ceremonial subterfuge, since the demon by means of this empty ritual impresses a sense of his own power upon his worshippers, and thus he ministers to his accursed pride. Moreover the ointment is a mockery of the Holy Chrism which is used in certain Sacraments as well as at the Coronation of a King. In the same way the staff or broom is just an empty adjuvant, a common object which the devil causes to be utilized in these mysterious locomotions as a dark and infernal symbol, infusing as it were something of a ritual and liturgical nature into his beastly orgies.

In connexion with, and actually as an argument against, the levitation and aerial journeys of witches there is often cited a document conveniently known as the Canon Episcopi, which is found in the collections *On Ecclesiastical Discipline*, a manual for the use of the bishop in the course of diocesan visitations, put together by the famous Benedictine Abbot Regino of Prüm about the year 906, but which although doubtless very much older than Regino's own day certainly does not date back to the First orthodox plenary Synod of Ancyra (now Angora, Asia Minor), which was held in 314, and to which body it was rather unaccountably referred by many older commentators and legists.

The text of this much debated and highly debatable section runs as follows: "This too must by no means be passed over that certain utterly abandoned women, turning aside to follow

Satan, being seduced by the illusions and phantasmical shows of demons firmly believe and openly profess that in the dead of night they ride upon certain beasts along with the pagan goddess Diana and a countless horde of women, and that in those silent hours they fly over vast tracts of country and obey her as their mistress, whilst on certain other nights they are summoned to do her homage and pay her service." For some reason Burchard added Herodias to Diana, and the two names were maintained in later recensions. The canon continues to say that an immense number of people, deluded by this false opinion, take these things to be very true, and thus fall away from the Christian faith since they are persuaded that something having a divine nature and ineffable power exists other than the one true God. In fine they lapse into paganism.

We must not read more into the Canon Episcopi than it precisely states. The "abandoned women" whom it so sternly censures are not witches flying to a Sabbat, but poor self-deceived creatures whose guilt consists in honouring, trusting to, obeying, and (so they deem) accompanying as her handmaids a heathen goddess in her nightly coursing through the air. They sin, moreover, in stubbornly maintaining that these evil fantasies and fables, inspired by the Father of Lies, are actual experiences and events. These delusions, no doubt, are very bad and even idolatrous. But there is no sorcery. There has been no pact with Satan. There is no working of Black Magic, no casting of malefic spells, no killing men and cattle.

Bishop Peter Binsfield treats the whole question of the Canon Episcopi at length and clearly shows that it is not aimed at witches and the midnight transvections of sorcerers to the Sabbat, but that quite another sect of deluded women is intended. His arguments are too lengthy to recapitulate here, but they are conclusive.

Later in the seventeenth century when discussing the levitation of witches the learned Jacques D'Autun openly challenged the authority of the Canon Episcopi. He pertinently inquired at what Council of Ancyra was this law laid down? He quoted the authority of Saint Augustine to show that the historical Councils of Ancyra must be deemed irregular if they are to be regarded as having any higher status than a Synod, and some even lie under the suspicion of Arianism. In any case it was not a General Council of the Church assembled under Papal Authority, and accordingly it could not promulgate a dogma. This Canon has in fact, he concludes, come to serve as a shield for the scoffer and agnostic.

The actual ceremonies of the Sabbat at which the members of the coven have now arrived vary so much (as has indeed already been pointed out) that although the essential features of Satan's synagogue are intrinsically the same at all times and in all countries it is no easy matter to give a general account of assemblies which were marked by such confessed and multitudinous details. This has been commented upon by all the demonologists, and is especially emphasized by De Lancre who made a particular study of the Sabbat as it was held in the South of France at the beginning of the seventeenth century, and who obtained his information at first-hand from the scores of witches he examined.

The liturgy of darkness, indeed, is of its very essence opposed to the comely worship of God, wherein, as the Apostle bids, all things are to be done "decently and in order".

The Sabbat is always conducted by a President or Chief, who is at the more important and larger meetings the Grand Master of the Satanists, at lesser assemblies the coven-master (who may, of course, be also the Grand Master) or some other official. Not infrequently an intelligence of evil, a demon, assumes corporeal form and presents himself for the adoration of his besotted followers.

The proceedings commence with the ceremonial homage paid to the President by the company, for as the witches told Remy there was always one who was invested with the chief authority on the night of their assembly.

The witches worship him by genuflections and kneeling; by

bowing the body; by holding up their hands as in prayer; by grotesque and ridiculous gestures; by uttering aloud the most horrid blasphemies and imprecations; by calling upon the demon as god.

When they approach to adore him "Sometimes they bend their knees as suppliants, and sometimes stand with their backs turned, and sometimes kick their legs high up so that their heads are bent back and their chins point to the sky".

At the trial of Louis Gaufridi at Aix in 1611 amplest details concerning this homage were forthcoming. "The hagges and witches, who are people of a sordid and base condition, are the first that come to adore the Prince of the Synagogue, who is Lucifer's lieutenant, and he that now holdeth that place is Lewes Gaufridy," that is to say he was Grand Master of the district. "Next they goe and worship the Divell who is seated in a Throne like a Prince." This shows that not unseldom a demon in corporeal form was present at these Sabbats.

Collette Dumont, a Guernsey witch, confessed that the Sabbat commenced with the adoration of the Devil, and Isebell Le Moigne, a member of the same coven, described how the demon compelled his votaries to go down on their knees before him, adoring him and calling upon him with the words "Our great Master, help us!"

Mention of the obscene ritual kiss, "the kiss of shame," the gage of fealty, is universal, and it is clear that this ceremony was invariably insisted upon and most scrupulously exacted. Delrio writes how the orgies are governed by a demon, Lord of the Sabbat, who often appears in some monstrous form as a great he-goat with flaming eyes and the whole company in token of abject submission kiss his fundament. As a sign of completes t servitude, remarks Ludwig Elich, at their meetings the witches kiss the devil's posterior. Shadwell puts it bluntly enough: *All kiss the Devil's Arse.* Upon this he glosses: "Kissing the Devil's Buttocks is part of the homage they pay the Devil, as *Bodin* says Doctor *Edlin* did, a *Sorbon* Doctor." Guillaume Edeline, Prior of St. Germain-en-Laye, was executed in 1453 as a wizard. He confessed that he had done homage to Satan who appeared in the shape of a ram by kissing his buttocks with great reverence.

In 1393 Walter Langton, Bishop of Coventry and treasurer of Edward I, was accused of sorcery and of paying homage to Satan in this way. Amongst other accusations he was commonly defamed and delated for the crime of worshipping the Devil by kissing his posterior, and also "it is reported that he hath had frequent colloquies with evil spirits". A sentence passed upon a coven of exceptionally evil and dangerous sorcerers at Avignon in 1582 details their crimes, when amongst other charges it is said: "You did worship the Prince of Devils in deed and word as very God, and (fie, for very shame!) with the greatest reverence you did kiss with sacrilegious mouth his most foul and beastly posterior." When the Sabbat was held at the haunted church of North Berwick in 1590 the Devil awaited the arrival of the witches "in the habit or likeness of a man, and seeing that they tarried overlong he at their coming enjoined them all to a penance which was that they should kiss his Buttocks in sign of duty to him, which being put over the Pulpit bare, every one did as he had enjoined them". Another account has it: "Now efter that the devil had endit his admonitions he cam down out of the pulpit, and caused all the company to come and kiss his ers quhilk they said was cauld lyk yce." A French witch, Jeanne Bosdeau, in 1594, confessed to the Bordeaux judges, how at a rendezvous of more than sixty Satanists at Puy-de-Dôme a black goatish form presided. "They kiss'd his Backside, and pray'd that he would help them." A very rare tract of the fourteenth century tells how the Waldenses in their secret synagogues adored a demon cat, whom they kissed under his tail.

The ceremonial offering and burning of candles at the Sabbat is often met with, and indeed these candles were something more than symbolic and a parody of the candles blessed by the Church since they were required for the very practical purpose of affording light at these midnight rendezvous. Guazzo tells us how the witches of North Italy presented "pitch black candles" to the devil; and Barthélemy Minguet, a French warlock, in his description of the Sabbat says that when the company went forward to adore their Master all of them were holding a pitch candle of black wax in their hands. These burned with a blue flame on account of the sulphurous material with which they were compounded. At the meeting of the Scotch witches at North Berwick round the pulpit whence the devil addressed his followers were set numbers of black tapers which burned smokily and with a blue light. Old Mother Styles told the Somersetshire magistrates that when she and her sister hags met the Man in Black "he delivers some Wax Candles like little Torches, which they give back again at parting".

It has already been pointed out that the devil-worshippers are greedy to draw others into the snare, and ever ready by most treacherous and foulest means to proselytize and betray others to their own damnation, activities which commend them mightily in the eyes of their master. When neophytes were received into this horrid society at the Sabbat the performance was conducted with much grotesque ritual and blasphemy. There was the formal pact; the repudiation of all good; the mock baptism with the infernal sponsors; the acceptance of the duties to be engaged in all mischief; the vows of silence and secrecy; the promise to recruit with diligence.

Instructions were also given to the society; death and destruction were plotted; plans were discussed and developed. Thus we find the North Berwick devil (the Grand Master) harangues his covens from the pulpit; the Pendle witches assemble at Malking Tower to contrive the deaths of their enemies; Alice Duke, Ann Bishop, Mother Penny, and the rest of the Somersetshire gang are instructed in the art of moulding wax pictures and transfixing them with thorns and pins; spells were taught orally; sometimes drugs and poisons were confected; the witch midwives learned the practice of abortion and the quality of emmenagogic savin. If these failed they resorted to surer swifter means. A witch who was executed at Dann in Switzerland "confessed that she had killed more than forty children, by sticking a needle through the crown of their heads into their brains, as they came out of the womb." Another witch-midwife of Strassburg said that she had killed more children than she could count.

Not infrequently high politics were the Question at these Sabbats, and the more powerful witches strove to decide the fate of countries and the lot of kings. It is undeniable that many of the wars which have convulsed nations, the broils and unrest, the revolutions that trouble and vex the world to-day, are in the first place organized by and energetically assisted by Satanists. For "rebellion is as the sin of witchcraft".

Lambert Daneau writes that Satan assembles his subjects at these devilish synagogues in order that he may examine them and understand with what diligence and success they have carried out their duties of harm and hurt to man and beast, whom they have injured, and what deaths they have contrived. The witch whose deeds are vilest and most abominable is the most highly honoured and applauded. Those, on the contrary, who have done no evil, are beaten and punished.

Thus Isobel Gowdie, the Scotch witch, gave a very ample account of how the devil or Grand Master tyrannized over the local coven. "He would beat and buffet us very sore," she complained. "We were beaten if we were absent from any gathering, or if we neglected to do anything he had commanded us." When Isebell Le Moigne, the Guernsey witch, on one occasion refused to accompany the familiar to James Gallienne's house, he returned to her in the shape of a man and bruised her severely about the face and head.

Strict discipline was observed among the Vaudois witches of Arras, and when one of the coven, Jean Tacquet, a rich eschevin, was minded to withdraw his allegiance from Satan, the demon forced him to continue it by thrashing him most cruelly with a bull's pizzle. As in the days of Remy, the Satanists even now bind themselves by a solemn oath never to betray their confederates. Any possible treachery to the infernal society constitutes, of course, the gravest offence in their eyes, and the modern Satanists stop at nothing to silence a traitor. To-day many members of these hellish leagues are only prevented from breaking away through fear. It is, as we might expect, a system of terrorism. Death is the penalty for any defection from their ranks, for naturally they are extremely reluctant that any hint of their dark secrets shall be revealed to the world. Nor are those whose aim it is to engineer universal anarchy and red revolution likely to shrink from a mere casual murder.

The business (so to speak) of the Sabbat having been dispatched, there followed the pleasures, which, as may well be supposed, were of the foulest and grossest kind. They mainly consisted in dancing and feasting. Sometimes they dance before eating and sometimes after the repast. The dances are generally performed in a circle and always round to the left, withershins, nor are they graceful and elegant movements, but the most erratic and ungainly caperings, jiggings and leapings, which prove wearisome beyond words, so what is ordinarily a pastime and a source of lawful amusement becomes a labour and a toil. Nor will the demon excuse any from the dance; those who are old and torpid he drives on until perforce they endeavour to stir their limbs, awkwardly and painfully enough, no doubt. So the notorious warlock parson, Mr. Gideon Penman, showed himself particularly active during the Sabbat rites, and "was in the rear in all their dances, and beat up all those that were slow".

The witches, according to Boguet, dance in a ring back to back, and he adds: "Sometimes too, although seldom, they dance in couples, and then one partner is here, another there, for always everything is higgledy-piggledy, in rank riot and confusion." De Lancre writes of the witches' revels that they "only dance three kinds of brawls. . . . The first is *à la Bohémienne* . . . the second with quick trippings: these are the round dances". In the third the dancers were placed one behind another in a long straight line. The brawls (French *le bransle*) was an old French dance resembling a cotillion.

In Belgium this witches' dance was known as *Pavana*.

During the Fian trial Agnes Sampson confessed that at North Berwick church above a hundred persons "danced along the *Kirk-yard*, *Geillis Duncan* playing on a Trump [Jew's harp], and *John Fian* mussiled [masked] led the *Ring*". As they danced, hand in hand, they were all singing with one voice,

> Cummer, go ye before, cummer, go ye,
> Gif ye will not go before, cummer, let me.

"These confessions made the King [James I, then James VI of Scotland] in a wonderful admiration, and he sent for the said Geillis Duncan, who, upon the like trump, did play the said dance before the King's Majesty."

The Capuchin Jacques D'Autun in his encyclopædic treatise on magic (*The Folly of the Wise and the Wisdom of the Simple*) speaks of sorcerers who gyrate hand in hand in a circle as if inspired by maniac frenzy.

He further remarks that whereas a dance should be distinguished by propriety and decorum, by a certain stateliness or it may be by lively frolic, the dances of witches are uncouth and ugly, extravagant and lewd. Such are the dances of savages, and it is worth remark that among the North American Indians there is but one word to express both dancing and coitus. Meanwhile the whole company are whooping and howling, hissing and yelling, in an access of horrid rage that is akin to an absolute frenzy.

There is evidence that various instruments accompanied the dance. Violins, flutes, tambourines, citterns, hautboys, and in Scotland the pipes made music at the Sabbat. Those of the witches who had any skill were called upon to perform, and very often they obliged the company with favourite airs of a vulgar kind, but the concert always ended in hideous cacophony and bestial clamour. In North Italy the covens were wont to "sing in honour of the devil the most obscene songs to the sound of a bawdy pipe and tabor played by one seated in the fork of a tree George Sinclar in his *Satan's Invisible World Discovered* says: "A reverend Minister told me, that one who was the Devils Piper, a wizzard confest to him, that at a Ball of dancing, the Foul spirit taught him a Baudy song to sing and play, as it were this night, and ere two days past all the Lads and Lasses of the town were lilting it throw the street. It were abomination to rehearse it." At Tranent in 1659 one man witch and eight women witches confessed that they had merry meetings with Satan, enlivened with music and dancing. John Douglas, the warlock, was the piper, and the two favourite airs of the Grand Master were "Kilt thy coat, Maggie, and come thy way with me", and "Hulie the bed will fa' ".

At Aix the witches danced "at the sound of Viols and other instruments, which are brought thither by those that were skilled to play upon them". None the less the sorcerers and hags joined in a kind of howling music with raucous cries imitating song. The Somerset witches of the Wincanton covens said that "The Man in black, sometimes playes on a Pipe or Cittern, and the company dance".

The music in fine was of many kinds, varying from harmonies "softly sweet, in Lydian measures", voluptuous and venereal, to the most horrid cacophony resembling the modern jazz, wherein (be it noted) some acute observers have shrewdly scented the devil's own orchestra. Fr. Philip De Ternant, writing in *The Universe*, 18th August, 1933, justly and in good time condemns the "Voodoo Cult imported into our Dance Sails without protest", and points out how young people are being corrupted by "the roll and the thump of the Voodoo Drum" which "responsive to subtle manipulation not far removed from black magic, plays a most hypnotic part" in the obscene, murderous, and wholly diabolical Voodoo cult. Quite unwittingly, no doubt, to-day many dancers are exercising their steps to the music of the witches. "Dreary pushing and pulling about the floor with almost aimless steps have now taken the place of dancing."

It was not without sound reason that Toussaint l'Ouverture when declaring the independence of Haiti and giving the Island a constitution forbade the Voodoo drum with its syncopation and sub-human appeal. The accursed thing has found a most profligate and tortuous entry in our midst, and unless recognized and sternly checked the poison will infect, rot, and fester, for such is its deliberate and appointed aim.

As the music of the witches, always evil, always unclean, varied in many modes so the feasts and banquetings of the witches were very dissimilar and differed widely both in their meats, their appointments, and also as regards the actual spots where they took place. According to the climate and customs of the country and the seasons of the year the Sabbat with its feast might be held under cover or in the open. Thus, as we should expect, in Italy and in France the Sabbat was frequently celebrated out of doors; in Guernsey the feast was usually spread on the sea-shore near Rocquaine Castle; in Sweden the witches met at a "place or house" under a roof; the Scotch covens assembled for the junketings in outbuildings, farms, in remote and deserted chapels; in warm weather the Riding Mill witches forgathered at the bridge end and on the moors, in colder seasons at Riding House, in a cellar or a barn; the Somersetshire witches made their rendezvous at Anne Bishop's cottage, and in the summer on the common hard by the village, or in a clearing of Selwood Forest.

In the etching of the Sabbat orgies by Jan Ziarnko, which illustrates De Lancre's great work (1612), witches and familiars are grouped round a table, and Spranger (1710) presents the Sabbat in very similar detail. In both these the horrid banqueters are seen eagerly devouring the limbs of a roasted babe. An old woodcut (1489) shows three witches seated at a board replenished with food and wine, whilst Guazzo depicts a numerous company at tables duly covered with neat napery and heaped with all sorts of dishes, which are busily served by a retinue of inferior demons. Sometimes, indeed, the cloths appear to have been spread on the ground, picnic fashion.

The accounts of the feast vary from one extreme to the other. The Milanese witches said that "all who have sat down to such tables are bound to allow that the feasts are foul and stinking, so that they nauseate the most ravenously hungry stomach. All sorts of food may be seen, but so vile and dirty and ill-dressed that the plates were not worth eating". Nicolas Morele said that the taste was so dry and bad that he was fain spue out the bits he had taken. "Their wine also is black like stale blood, and is given to the company in some filthy sort of drinking horn. There is plenty of everything save only white bread and salt".

This is all very concisely summed up in the great work of the theological school of the University of Salamanca, usually quoted as "the Salamanca doctors": "The witches make a meal from food either furnished by themselves or by the Devil. It is sometimes most delicious and delicate, and sometimes a pie baked from babies they have slain, or disinterred corpses. A suitable grace is said before such a table". Thus when Isobel Gowdie, of Auldearne (1662), described the feast of her society which took place in Grangehill she gave fullest details: "The Devil sat at the head of the table, and all the Coven about. That night he desired Alexander Elder in Earlseat to say the grace before meat, which he did; and is this:—

> We eat this meat in the Devil's name,
> With sorrow, and sighing, and mickle shame;
> We shall destroy house and hold,
> Both sheep and beeves within the fold.
> Little good shall come to the fore
> Of all the rest of the little store.

And then we began to eat. And when we had ended eating, we looked steadfastly to the Devil, and bowing ourselves to him, we said to the Devil, We thank thee, our Lord, for this." The giving thanks to the Devil at the finish of the banquet appears to be practically a universal custom. Delrio remarks that he had actually seen and read the formulas for the "devil's grace" before and after meat. They were written out on parchment by a sorcerer constant in his attendance at Sabbats. "The grace said at this table is worthy of the infernal crew. In phrases of hideous profanity they acknowledge Beelzebub as the creator and giver and preserver of all the gifts they receive, and in the same strain do they return thanks to the foul spirit when they arise after having eaten and the tables are removed."

It has been already noticed that Ziarnko and Spranger depict the covens as feasting in cannibal fashion on human limbs, and Dominique Isabelle, a witch of Rogeville, confessed to Remy that she had seen and tasted the flesh of babes at the devil's table. At the trial of Louis Gaufridi in 1610 it came to light that the flesh of young children "which they cook and make ready in the Synagogue" was served to the witches. Madeleine Bavent also describes how on a Good Friday "the assembly performed a horrible mockery of the Last Supper. They brought the body of an infant who had been roasted, and this was eaten by them all". Sometimes human meat was eaten for magical purposes. The witches were adepts at child-stealing, or if they failed to kidnap they would not hesitate to kill their own infants. The flesh was often seethed in a caldron until it became potable, when it was regarded as a charm of surpassing power. Hence a witch busy at her caldron, confecting these horrible ingredients, so often appears in illustrations, as for example the engraved frontispiece to the rare 1656 edition (often called an Elzevir) of a work on *Magic, Ghosts, and Apparitions of all kinds*, issued by Hennig Grosse, a well-known publisher of Leipzig. Thus the Parisian witches of the Guibourg and La Voisin covens in the days of Louis XIV murdered from first to last literally hundreds of "unwanted" babies at their devilish rites, and were supplying at a high price philtres and potions of these horrible ingredients to a vast number of eager clients. A Moorish sorceress will dig up a newly-buried corpse, set it before her between her legs, and guiding the clay-cold hands stirs with them *cousscouss* (granulated flour steamed over broth) which thus acquires certain magical properties, as a love-charm, or more often when mixed with earth from a grave and certain filthy ingredients becomes the *taam*, or "accursed food", a slow but certain poison if only but a few grains be swallowed.

MAGIC, GHOSTS AND PHANTOMS
"*Magica de Spectris*" by Hennig Grösse

Nicolas Remy and very many other authorities emphasize the fact that salt never appears at the witches' table. Bodin says that salt as an emblem of eternity is hateful to the demon; and a German writer, Philip Ludwig Elich, is most careful to point out that salt is never seen at these evil banquets. It were easy to accumulate a mass of evidence from the witches' confessions in reference to this detail, but it will suffice to observe that in England and Scotland this taboo does not appear, the reason being that in Catholic countries salt is sanctified in solemn sacrament and ceremonial, since the ritual employs two kinds of salt for liturgical purposes, the baptismal salt and the blessed salt exorcized in the preparation of holy water from which devils flee. Salt is blessed again for the use of animals, and in honour of St. Hubert. It is used in the consecration of a church. From the earliest days indeed it has had a sacred and religious character. Protestant England knew nothing of all this.

The food furnished at Sabbats in the British Isles was for the most part seemingly of good quality and satisfying, but seldom of any extraordinary kind. The Forfar coven in 1661 at Mary Rynd's house made themselves merry with strong March ale and brandy. The Auldearne society met at a house where they had beef in plenty, ale and other good drink. The Somersetshire witches who met on Lie Common, "all sate down, a white Cloth being spread on the ground, and did drink Wine, and eat Cakes and Meat." Some ten years later the Riding Mill company were sumptuously regaled with boiled capons, cheeses, butter, flour, beef, bottles of wine and "a variety of meat". The devil enticed the poorer sort of Swedish witches "by presenting them with Meat and Drink", and at their rendezvous, Blockula, which was evidently a large country house, they sat down at a very long table whereon were "Broth with Colworts and Bacon in it, Oatmeal, Bread spread with Butter, Milk and Cheese. And they added that sometimes it tasted very well, and sometimes very ill".

www.ingramcontent.com/pod-product-compliance
Lightning Source LLC
Chambersburg PA
CBHW030123170426
43198CB00009B/725